I0164504

Volunteer Kids

Ideas to Get You Started

By Brandi Brown

A publication of Rekindled Media

Printed in the United States of America

First Rekindled Media Printing, 2015

Rekindled Media
P.O. Box 41272
Raleigh, NC 27629

www.brandibrownonline.com

Never doubt that you can change the world! There's no one better to do it than you!

- Brandi

Introduction

"Volunteer" is such a big word, but the spirit of volunteerism doesn't have to be scary. Being a volunteer simply means that you do something for others for free without expecting to get anything in return. Seasoned volunteers – people who have been doing volunteer work for many years – will tell you, however, that volunteer experiences often bring something happy to our lives. When we volunteer and know that we are helping other people, it makes us feel good inside. There have been many times in my life when I have been overjoyed when I have seen the outcome of a volunteer effort, and I know that you can feel that way, too.

Some people think that "being a volunteer" has to mean making an agreement to do something for a long time or that it has to be "official" and a serious task. In the world of volunteering, you will find that it just isn't true! While official volunteers who work on a set schedule, such as volunteers who help to walk dogs at animal shelters, definitely are needed, there are plenty of impromptu, or "spur of the moment" volunteer jobs waiting right around the corner. You can make up your own volunteer projects, too!

When I was in college, one of my friends knew that a local shelter that housed homeless women and their children had to get rid of their swing set. It was broken and dangerous, but the shelter's budget did not include the money for a new one. This particular friend was an artist, and her idea was to use that to raise the money for a swing. She got friends to let her borrow their paintings for the night. She cleared out the furniture in her living room and hung the paintings. She told everyone she knew about the fundraising art exhibit. At the event, she sold bottles of water and soft drinks and had donations buckets at every door. With just a few days' worth of work, she managed to raise enough for the new swing set and a slide for the shelter! That kind of volunteer project can feel almost electric because it is so exciting, and it benefits many people for years to come.

In the pages that follow, you will find 75 ideas for volunteer projects. They are not the only ideas out there! In fact, you can use these ideas to help you come up with idea that suit your interests and abilities.

Quick Ideas

Help out at the local soup kitchen.

Soup kitchens are a great first stop for volunteers. Common jobs include helping with setting tables by putting out napkins and utensils; ensuring that trash cans are available; greeting people who come by for a meal; and serving food. If you are older than 12, you may be able to help prepare some food dishes as well. Check with local churches, particularly local Catholic churches, for opportunities to assist or contact your local homeless shelter for the locations of soup kitchens in your area. Most of them are open for 1-2 hours for lunch and another 2-hour block for an evening meal.

> **DID YOU KNOW?**
> As of 2013 (the last date for which we have numbers), there were more than 610,000 people in the United States who are homeless. How many homeless people are in your town?

Sort items for the food pantry.

When items come into food pantries, they typically come in mixed up in bags or boxes. The food pantry employees then use volunteers to help sort those bags and boxes into categories. In a well-organized food pantry, the shelves will be labeled clearly so that the canned food section will have a space for green beans, carrots, tuna, etc. while the bagged area will have spots for white rice, brown rice, beans, and other foods. Because of the highly organized nature of most food pantries, sorting and shelving food is an excellent way to volunteer for people as young as three or four years old.

Play with dogs at the animal shelter.

Animal shelters often run with only a few people who are paid to work there. That means animal shelters, and the animals that live there, depend on people who volunteer. Most shelters have strict guidelines for how old people must be before they can volunteer and what they can do. One job that is in high demand is dog walking. The dogs at the shelter will need to be walked each day, and it takes many volunteers to do this job. If you want to walk dogs, check out shelters in your area and ask about what you need to do in order to help out.

Help sort items for food programs for low-income students.

Many students in schools with high numbers of low-income students have programs like Backpack Buddies. These programs involve school staff members collecting food through donations and then sorting the food into bags to send home with children in food insecure homes. While the names of students who are in these programs are kept private, there may be opportunities to assist with the program by sorting the food and putting it into bags for staff members to hand out. As an extended volunteer opportunity, consider trying to get other students to rotate to help out each week.

Make treats for your teachers.

Making treats for teachers can be as easy or hard as you want it to be. A nice card that you make as a thank you can be a very kind action to take. Making brownies, cookies, or other sweet treats also is a good way to show your teacher that you like her class, but another option is to make something that your teacher can use in his classroom. For example, making bookmarks that your teacher can give to students, customized pencil boxes, or tote bags for school supplies also can be wonderful gifts to make for your teacher.

Give your bus driver something for Bus Driver Appreciation.

Bus Driver Appreciation Week occurs at different times in various states. (Have an adult help you do a web search for your state.) If you ride the bus to or from school, there are several ways that you can show thanks to your bus driver. A card or piece of your driver's favorite fruit can be great choices. Also consider doing something cute like a small stop sign saying "I want to 'STOP' and say thanks" attached to a jar or bag of goodies. Small gestures often are very much appreciated by people who don't usually get a "thank you" for their job. Your bus driver gets you to school and home safely, and that's a very important job!

Pack meal baskets for Thanksgiving.

Churches, homeless shelters, and soup kitchens are among the places that plan out Thanksgiving food baskets. These baskets usually have everything for a tasty Thanksgiving dinner – turkey, sweet potatoes, cranberry sauce, green beans, and maybe even some sparkling juice. As a volunteer, your job would be to put the right food in each basket and help to wrap it up, usually with plastic wrap and a bow. Others will volunteer to help out by driving the baskets that you pack to the people who need them. You will get the opportunity to help others have a great holiday!

Make posters for your school's PTA.

One of the many ways that school PTAs are able to get the word out for events and activities that are happening is to put up posters at the front door to the school as well as in popular hallways like outside the cafeteria or bathrooms. Volunteer by yourself or with a group of friends to get together after school and make posters. This task is perfect for artistic students and takes a job off the shoulders of parents and can help you to get involved with making your school's events successful.

Help set up your school's book fair.

While students are not allowed to help sell books during the book fair because of the money involved, that doesn't mean that you cannot help out in other ways! For example, you can ask if you can help to set up books during the day before the book fair. In most cases, the books come in heavy boxes and are marked with categories, but you may be able to assist adults with putting the books out on the table. You also could set up tables with flyers and other information for students who attend the book fair. Ask your school's librarian or media center specialist who is in charge of your school's book fair and then contact that person about helping out.

Clean up your school's playground.

A clean-up of your school's playground is one of the simplest ways that you can make your school grounds better. Talk to a couple of teachers who you think may be interested in helping out. All you will need to do is have those teachers set up a time for their students to pick up an area of the school grounds. Try to find parents or local business leaders who will provide trash cans and gloves. Deliver them to the teachers on the morning of the school pick-up. If there is an interest, you also may be able to set up a continuous cleaning throughout the school year to keep the grounds in good shape.

Make art for a school auction.

School auctions are a perfect place for students of all ages to participate in helping to earn money for their schools. Does your school have an annual auction as a fundraiser? If so, find out who is in charge and ask that person if you can create artwork that gets put up for auction. Do something that you believe people would be willing to pay to take home with them. Many school auctions begin as low as $5 for initial bidding, but it's possible that a quality piece of student artwork could sell for $20 or more, which can help with making money for your school.

Make a card for a sick relative.

When you have a relative, whether it's an aunt, uncle, grandma, grandpa, or cousin, who is sick, an easy way to brighten that person up is to make your own card to send. Draw something pretty and write a special note to the sick relative. You can spruce up these letters by adding in some jokes or fun puzzles. You may want to purchase some stickers for younger relatives or include a book or other trinket for older relatives. Handmade cards are one of the best gifts that you can give to someone you love who has been ill.

Offer to take out trash for an elderly neighbor.

Do you have an older neighbor or one who is sick? Offering to take out the trash, especially if you already take out your own family's trash, is an easy way to make a big difference in someone's life. Just head over and say something like, "Hi, Ms. Diaz. I noticed that you seem to have to work hard to get your big trash can to the curb each week. I would be happy to bring it out when I bring ours out." Although it may take you only 5 minutes each week, doing this task could take a large amount of stress off your neighbor's weekly schedule.

Donate your old toys.

Donating old toys is one of the easiest ways that you can help someone else out. When you have outgrown a toy, put it in a box marked for donation. Ask an adult if you can keep this box of items to donate the basement, garage, or another place that will be out of the way but still easy to access. Goodwill and The Salvation Army are two good places for toy donations, but homeless shelters, children's centers, and even children's hospitals can be good spots to donate as well. Make a big effort just before Christmas and again when school lets out for the summer to get rid of any toys that you no longer need or want.

Donate your old books.

There are plenty of places where you can take your old books once you have outgrown them. Consider giving them to a family friend or a relative who has children younger than you. Also ask at your place of worship, doctor or dentist office, and other places where children gather. Many of these locations are in need of items to keep children busy while they wait, but they don't have the budget to buy much. Even animal shelters often need books and toys for children who are waiting for their parents to complete a pet adoption.

Sort books for a book sale.

> **DID YOU KNOW?**
>
> The United Way reports about one-quarter of Americans donate some of their time each year. That means about 75 million people will help a cause or group. Will you be in that group this year?

Many public libraries have book sales as a way to raise funds. If your library has an annual sale, ask if they accept children or youth volunteers. One of the main tasks of this kind of fundraiser is to sort the books into categories. For example, all cookbooks, children's books, mystery novels, and other types of books would go together to make it easier for people to purchase items at the book sale. These jobs often require more volunteers than the library has, and the organizers may be happy to have extra hands to assist.

Collect books for a book drive.

Another way to volunteer when it comes to books is to collect books for a local book drive – or even plan your own drive! You can collect books from relatives, friends, neighbors, or even other kids at school. Have a place where you plan to take the books once they are collected. Then you will need to set out bins and let people know about your book collection. Try to set a small goal, such as 50 books, and keep the bin updated with the number you have collected. Once the drive is over, have a parent help you to transport the books to the location where they will be donated.

Collect gloves for others in the winter.

Winter is harsh for people who don't have the proper attire. A pair of gloves, even a thin pair, is much better for your hands than having them exposed to the elements. Ask your teacher if it would be possible to host a drive at school for gloves. Make posters to hang around your school and then tell everyone about your plan. Collect gloves from your classmates and then take them to a local homeless shelter or even to your town's social services department. Many people seek out help in the winter with gloves, coats, and scarves, and your donation could make a huge difference.

Help a younger child learn a skill.

As you get older, you will know how to do more than kids younger than you, and one way that you can help others is to offer to teach those children a skill that you know. If you are good at math, for instance, you may want to teach someone how to do addition and subtraction. Outside of academic skills, you could volunteer to teach a younger child how to trap a soccer ball, make a grilled cheese, or rake the yard. While teaching about these types of skills isn't typically what most people consider "volunteering," it's the kind of help that can make a real difference in a person's life.

Tutor a younger child.

Let's return to the idea of helping out with math skills. Offering to tutor a child in math, science, or reading can be a wonderful way to help improve someone's life. Think about it for a few seconds. A child who is struggling to read in second grade is already behind her peers. An older child or teen stepping in to help her out with individualized, free reading lessons could make a significant impact on her life now and in the future. Many elementary schools are in need of tutors and would be happy to set someone up with children who need help if you contact the school and ask.

Help out at your school's carnival.

School carnivals are awesome fun, but they are tons of work as well! Planning and executing a school carnival typically takes hundreds of volunteer hours, and on the day of the event, there are plenty of jobs to do from staffing welcome tables to collecting tickets for the popcorn booth. Contact the organizer of your school's carnival to find out if there are jobs that are kid-friendly that you could help do. Some ideas may be helping with set up and clean up, running a ticket-free booth, painting faces, or giving directions to people who need help finding where to go.

Do laundry at your local animal shelter.

Did you know that animal shelters produce several loads of laundry a day? Yes, they do! All of the animals living in the shelter use bedding, pillows, and even sheets. Sick animals being cared for in the shelter often go through many loads of laundry each day. The need for people to volunteer to wash and fold that laundry is pretty significant because most shelters couldn't stay caught up even if they had someone washing linens 24 hours a day. Find out if the shelter accepts children as volunteers to do this job. It's pretty simple, and it's a great way to get started doing a much-needed task.

Set up a small educational library at your local animal shelter.

"Tiny libraries" are becoming a trend throughout the United States. A tiny library is one that fills a certain niche, a small subject area. Animal shelter workers often work hard to educate the public about how to care for their pets, especially if people adopt breeds like pit bulls or less common household pets like rabbits and guinea pigs. Putting together a tiny library, which usually has fewer than 50 books, requires some type of holding case and the books. The idea is that the books are free to take and read for anyone who is interested with the hope that they will be returned. In a place like an animal shelter, people would be able to read the book at the shelter or check them out if the shelter workers would like to go that route.

Volunteer to change the kitty litter at your local animal shelter.

Working with cats and kittens at the animal shelter is one of the jobs that children are the most likely to be permitted to do. Changing kitty litter isn't a fun task. It's one that even many people who love their cats do not want to do, but it needs to be done in order to keep the cats in a clean environment. Coming in to clean kitty litter is a task that only takes about 30 minutes even in large shelters and needs to be done twice a day, making this volunteer opportunity one that works well for young volunteers.

Pack donated school supplies for children who need it.

Around the time that school starts each year, many businesses and organizations ask their members and customers to donate pencils, notebook paper, folders, and other supplies for local schools. Someone then packs those supplies, often into backpacks, to deliver to children at specific schools. Connect with someone you know who is involved with one of the businesses or organizations in your local area that conducts a drive and ask if you can come in to help with packing those supplies before delivery.

Offer to babysit for a family in crisis.

When a family is dealing with a tragedy, people often bring food and offer to provide transportation or even cleaning. Another job people often need in a crisis is someone to stay with small children while the adults get a break or deal with the tragedy. Even if a family has elementary-aged children, teens can offer to hang out with them for a couple of hours. Parents will appreciate this type of gesture because they often have paperwork and other items to take care of and could use the small break from their children to get more done efficiently.

Visit a local nursing home.

Nursing homes often have residents who have very few visitors. One of the best uses of your volunteer time if you are extroverted, meaning that you enjoy spending time with and talking to people, is to spend time with people who are living in nursing homes and may not have much interaction with other people. You can offer to read to people who are losing their eyesight or play board games with people who may be interested in spending some time with someone young and energetic. You should call the resident coordinator before attending. This person's job is to make sure that the residents have activities to keep them busy. This person can give you the details of how volunteering works and help to connect you   with   the   right   person.

Adopt a grandparent.

"Adopt A Grandparent" programs are formal in some areas. If your town has such a program, which you could find using a Google search, contact the person who is in charge in order to find out how you sign up. Without a formal program, you still could contact your minister, rabbi, imam, or other worship leader to find out about older adults who may need company. These programs help you to connect with people in public places to visit local sites of interest, read books together, and generally make a personal connection.

Plan a local park cleanup.

Local park cleanups are simple to plan and require very little in terms of resources. All you will need to do is gather latex gloves, sharp sticks (for poking trash on the ground), and trash bags. You can do a park cleanup on your own and simply head out for an hour to pick up trash in a small area of the park. You could commit to cleaning up this area of the park each month or quarter if you want an on-going project. Also, you could convince some friends or neighbors to come out as well and get a larger part of the park cleaned up.

Plant something at local parks.

This one definitely requires permission and parent assistance. If you have noticed areas of your local park that are devoid of trees and could use the shade, have an adult help you to contact your town's parks department. They may be willing to allow you to plant trees that are easy to maintain, especially if you can commit to maintaining them over the next five to 10 years. Then you just need to purchase the trees – or have a local nursery donate them – and head out to do the planting. Be sure to research the best trees to plant in your area.

Participate in an Arbor Day planting.

Arbor Day is a holiday that serves to encourage groups to focus on tree planting and maintenance. Many civic groups, like the Rotary Club or Kiwanis Club, have tree-planting ceremonies in which they plant trees in certain places. Arbor Day plantings may occur on public grounds like parks, but they often are in private locations, such as for a seating area outside a hospital for guests to relax. Arbor Day is the third Friday in April in the United States, and if you want to help out on this day, start looking for local ads in March. You also may ask adults to keep an ear out for word of Arbor Day celebrations in your town.

Make hospital activity bags.

Hospitals can be boring! They are boring for patients, whether young or old, especially if those patients are not able to move around much. They also can be painfully boring places for young children to hang out if a parent or sibling is in the hospital. A hospital activity bag may have puzzle books, a deck of cards, and local magazines, or even a stress ball for adults while children's activity books can include small puzzles, handheld or travel games (like Connect Four, checkers, Uno, or Old Maid),

Learn More: Little Free Library

The state of Wisconsin is home to the Little Free Library, an organization that jumpstarted the tiny library movement in America. The "tiny library movement" is a more generic name used to describe these set-ups. These libraries and information about them goes by other names, too, including pop-up libraries, micro-libraries, neighborhood book exchanges, and even book trading posts.

The idea behind Little Free Library is simple. Even free public libraries may not be available to everyone. Instead, a tiny library can help alleviate this concern. A tiny library is very small, sometimes just the size of a bird feeder, and may house anywhere from 10 to 50 books on a specific topic.

A Little Free Library works well if the books are centered around a certain topic, but that certainly does not have to be the case. All that is required is that you find a space where you have permission to host the library, the container, and the initial books!

If you want to be connected with the Little Free Library organization, visit them online at http://www.littlefreelibrary.org.

and crayons and coloring books. If you make hospital activity bags, ask at the front desk about where you can deliver them, and if you are willing to make more, leave your name and phone number.

Participate in a Walk or Fun Run.

Charity walks or runs are a wonderful idea for many reasons and are the perfect place for young children and teens to learn about giving back! The people who put together these runs often are volunteering their time, and all of the money paid for entry fees goes toward the charity the run is supporting. Entry fees range from $15-$30 in most small cities and towns, and the race coordinators will advertise where the money is going. Participating allows you to keep your body in great shape while donating money to a good cause.

Clean up the neighborhood.

Your neighborhood probably has some spots that could use cleaning. Unless you have a neighborhood grounds crew that is able to get to every nook and cranny of the streets, there are likely to be bits of trash scattered along with debris that has blown away in a storm or other items that need to be cleaned up. There is no need for any planning here. Just head out on a Saturday afternoon with a trash bag and pick up anything that looks easy and safe to pick up.

Put inspirational bookmarks in donated books.

Are you planning to do Volunteer Idea #15 – donate your old books? One way to add a little pizzazz to this project is to make inspirational bookmarks and put them in the books for the person who buys them. Go to a website (with an adult's permission) such as www.BrainyQuote.com or www.QuoteGarden.com and pick out a few sayings that you think could make people feel better. Cut cardstock into strips that are 2 inches wide by 4 inches long. Use paint, markers, or stickers to decorate the bookmarks and put the quotes in nice lettering on the bookmark as well. Then just slip them snugly into the books you plan to donate. You're sure to brighten someone's day!

Volunteer at a rescue farm.

Rescue farms are interesting, and slightly eccentric, places to donate your time. These farms usually are small operations; often the only people who work at the farm are the people who own it. The farmers take in animals that are sick or injured. They nurse some of them back to health and return them to the wild while others will live there permanently. After finding a rescue farm in your area, head out as a visitor. Check out the farm, and if you like it, you can offer to help out. Coming in with specific project ideas, such as a goat pen that looks like it needs mending, will be helpful but also be open to work that the farmers really need completed.

Read to others at a children's hospital.

Even if you are an early reader yourself, you can help to read to other children at a children's hospital. Toddlers just need someone who can share books that mostly have pictures. Teens can do more reading volunteerism, even reading to older adults who have trouble seeing. Contact the Volunteer Coordinator at your local hospital if you want to set up a time to come in to read. This type of volunteer program is good for both one-time events and an on-going volunteer effort. The best part about this type of volunteer work is that it gives a much-needed break to parents and other caregivers who strive to entertain patients who are stuck in the hospital.

Lead games at a homeless shelter.

Game night is a fun, inexpensive way to help others stay entertained. Often staying at homeless shelters can be a lonely –

even scary – existence. You can help to alleviate some of this fear by helping to coordinate a game night! Ask friends and neighbors if you can borrow their board games and decks of cards. (Be sure to mark everyone's property so that you can return it to the right person.) Set up a table of games to choose from for adults and be prepared to lead children in games, such as Candy Land, Left Right Center, or even outdoor games like hopscotch.

Collect razors for a men's shelter.

Men's shelters sometimes need donations more desperately than women's shelters. One of the reasons is that children also stay at women's shelters while kids typically are prohibited at men's shelters. That means getting donations can be easier because it is easier to collect donations for places where children are staying. If you want to make a difference in a really meaningful way at a men's shelter, collect razors to hand out. Men who are trying to find work or just want to feel better about their hygiene could use a steady supply of razors. Ask your father and other male relatives and neighbors if they are willing to donate a pack of their own razors if they buy them in packs. If not, try to get them to purchase a pack for you to donate.

Lead a cleanup at a local shelter.

When running any type of building where many people live, keeping the place clean is a constant struggle! Many shelters have rotating chores, similar to what many teachers have in classrooms, requiring the residents to help out. In what are called "emergency shelters," places where homeless people can live for up to 30 days, people aren't there enough to participate heavily in keeping it clean. Gather a group of five to six friends who are hard workers and plan a cleaning party at a local shelter. (Call ahead to schedule it, of course!) Go in with a plan to clean a specific area, such as one common living room or all of the hallways. Don't overdo it, but you can plan to return quarterly if you would like to help out more.

Lead a beautification project at a local shelter.

Beautification projects typically refer to outdoor projects. Making a place look good can change the outlook of the folks who live there – and make the workers feel happier, too! Find someone who works in landscaping who will help you out. Come up with a plan with a sketch of the yard and what plants would be good to use. Look for plants that require little maintenance and will live for years. Then contact local nurseries and hardware stores to ask people for donations of plants. Work with the volunteer coordinator at the shelter to help you find people who will participate in doing the yard work for you. Remember that these projects often take place in phases, and it's okay to do only a bit of the work each spring until it's completed.

Read newspapers to the elderly.

Much like reading books in the hospital, reading to the elderly can be a great way for you to practice a skill while helping someone else out. While books are fun, reading the newspaper is more important for some elderly people because they want to be able to keep up with what is going on in the world. This type of volunteer effort is best at nursing homes where many people are still mentally sound but just are not able to read because of poor eyesight or shaky hands. Offer to come in for an hour a week to read important news stories to help keep the residents informed on current events.

Set up chairs for an event.

This simple task can save adults much headache! When your school or church has a special event, someone has to drag out chairs and set them up for the audience. This job can take a while and be physically taxing because some events need hundreds of chairs. Lend a hand! Helping to carry out chairs even for 10 minutes can lift the load off a probably already overburdened adult volunteer force. Before a major event, ask the adult in charge if you can help with chairs and recruit a couple of friends to help as well. If four adults were planning to set up, and you have four teens who help out, that cuts the workload in half!

Plan a simple welcome back event for teachers.

Sometimes parent organizations plan large welcome back events for teachers, which is wonderful. A simple student-led plan can be great as well, however, especially if your school's parent organization typically does not have an event. Many breakfast places will donate coffee, bagels, or pastries to a school event. Start asking about three weeks before the event to see if you can find any donations. Come in on a day when teachers have a workday (when they are setting up their rooms before the school year begins) and set out the spread in the teachers' lounge. For non-food welcome back gifts, try writing a small card for each teacher or bringing in school supplies with "thank you" notes attached to them.

Grow extra veggies to give away.

Does your family grow a garden? Even if you have a container garden or a couple of rows planted in your backyard, you can help. Just one tomato plant can provide tomatoes for a single family over the harvest season. Ask your parents if you can set aside part of the family's plot, or expand it, to give fresh produce to a family you know that may need it. Fresh fruits and veggies have enormous nutritional benefits that many low-income families cannot afford.

Make snack baskets for sick friends.

When you have a friend who gets sick, pack a basket of goodies to take over! Think about the things you would like to have when you are sick, such as tasty juices, new books, or a handheld toy. Get these items and send them to your friend with a get well note. Remember that your friend may not want company when she's sick, so have a parent call her to see if you can bring the goodies over, even if you have to give them to your friend's parent at the door.

Pack boxes of items to send to soldiers.

Even when soldiers are not at war, there are plenty of them who are in areas where they cannot have family live there with them. Ask around to connect with local soldiers' families to find out where there is a unit to which you can send a care package. Small items like playing cards and puzzle books are excellent choices as well as small snacks that will survive being transported internationally. You can pack a single box on your own or coordinate a drive among your friends and classmates to send more.

Give popsicles to people working outside.

Yes, you read this idea right! When you are working out in the sun, a nice Popsicle tastes delicious! Get your parents to buy a box of Popsicles when you go to the grocery store. Then give them out to people who are working in the hot sun. *(Always, always get an adult to go with you!)* People who are doing construction; police officers who work walking city streets; and garbage collectors who come to your neighborhood are good people to try.

Make autism magnets.

Autism Spectrum Disorder (ASD) is becoming more diagnosed in many communities. While people with autism often are high functioning, many of them have challenges with interacting with others, especially strangers. Help with this problem by making magnets to go on the cars or even front doors of people you know who have an autistic family member. "Please be patient. Someone with autism lives here." This statement is common for these kinds of magnets and just let others know that they may not receive a response to any random inquiry.

Give compliments freely!

One of the best and easiest ways to help people is just to give compliments to people! There is no special skill or early planning required. Simply tell people that you like something they are wearing or something they did. "I really loved the painting you did in class today" or "wow, those shoes are nice!" can help brighten someone's day. You never know when those little comments, sometimes called "random acts of kindness," will help to alter someone's outlook entirely. Someone who is having a difficult time feeling good about himself could need a simple compliment very badly. As you go about your day, remember to be kind to others as a way to let your volunteer spirit shine!

26

More Involved Ideas

Coordinate drive for humane society.

A drive does not have to be a complicated, involved endeavor. You can make a humane society drive as small or big as they want. The first step is to have a parent help you to contact the local animal shelter. Explain what you're doing and ask if there is anything that need really badly. Sometimes items like towels and kitty litter are donated less often than others.

Once you know what they need, make flyers or poster to advertise your drive. Decide who you will target. Perhaps you will want to ask neighbors. Maybe there is a church bazaar coming up, and you can set up a table there. Talk to everyone you know about donating to the humane society drive. Food and kitty litter typically are the items that every shelter needs most of the time.

Make business cards for your local shelter.

People who live in even small-sized cities know that there are often homeless people around grocery stores, entertainment venues, and other locations. While you may not want to give those people money, there are other ways to help. One way is to print up business cards with information letting people know the contact information for the local shelter.

The cost for this type of project is minimal. You can purchase business card template paper at an office supply store for around $20. Then you can use a word processing program to design the business cards. (On Microsoft Word, go to the "Mailings" tab on the top toolbar. Then choose "Labels" and pick the style number of the cards you purchased.)

Once you have designed the cards, you can print as many copies as you'd like. If you have a printer at home, you should be able to do it there, but if not, you can bring your purchased cards into an office supply store to have them printed. Then keep these cards with you to give to people who may need to go to a shelter. Also, you could offer to keep the local police department, fire department, or even shelter office supplied with cards that the people there can give to anyone who may need it. Having the right information may be the difference between a warm bed and a night on the streets for many people who find themselves homeless.

Make a tiny library in your neighborhood.

The Little Free Movement is a nationwide trend in the United States. Find a place and get permission to put up a tiny library. These "libraries" are only about 4 feet by 4 feet wide, meaning that they do not take up much space. The area where the library will be should be a place, such as a public park or on school property, accessible to everyone.

Once you have permission to put up the library, you will need to get the materials to construct the tiny library. Unless you are very handy, this part of the project will require some help from adults who are able to assist you in the construction process. The tiny library will need shelves that you will need to build into the unit or plan to purchase separately.

Finally, once you have your tiny library built, you will be able to begin the process of putting books in it. Ask your local librarian, as well as your school's librarian, for books that he or she may no longer want to keep in the library for circulation but that may work for your purposes. Also go to discount bookstores and garage sales to   find bargain books, and of course don't forget to ask friends for donations.

Plan a penny drive.

A penny drive is a good fundraiser for a school, and it is simple to plan. Decide on a project that you want to see come into fruition. Something in the range of $100-200 for many schools will be sufficient. Perhaps you want to purchase a new bench for outside of the school or a media center set of a popular book series. With your goal in mind, begin to plan the remainder of the penny drive

Collect one jar for each teacher or grade level, depending on how you want to organize the drive. You will make signs with the teacher/grade names and attach them to the jars. When you are advertising your penny drive, let students know that they should put their change (although dollars certainly are welcome as well!) into the jar for their class or grade level. The drive should last 1-2 weeks.

At the end of the drive, have someone help you count the money donated on each teacher's behalf. That class should win a small prize, such as getting to dismiss 5 minutes early one day or Popsicles for the class. The money then should go to the organization supporting your penny drive or directly to purchase the items for the project. Don't forget to announce whether you met your goal and let people know what their donations helped fund!

Put on a skit for local daycares.

Daycare centers frequently are looking for something to help them keep their little charges occupied. Offering to come in to provide free entertainment for the children can be a meaningful way to volunteer for you and a stress-reliever for them. People who love drama are ideal candidates for this type of volunteer project. Pick a simple children's story or come up with a story of your own.

Invite others who share this love for theatre to participate in the process. Spend time preparing the skit, making costumes, and designing an easily portable set. Then you can begin to contact daycare centers about whether they would be willing to allow you to come in to perform for them.

When you are invited to a daycare center, be certain to be respectful of the rules of the center. Perform your skit and then engage with the children who were in the audience. Ask what they liked and how they thought the story would end. Use their feedback to improve future performances and note that you are doing something meaningful and fun that can help other people to enjoy themselves.

Put together an in-house art show.

Do you remember when you read about an in-home art show in the introduction to this book? If you don't, go back to check it out now. The idea behind this volunteer project is the same. You will need to determine a local project that could use your help. Perhaps you want to raise money for cancer awareness or to buy new toys for an after-school program for impoverished youth. Once you have a project to fund and the cost, you will have your in-house art show's goal.

Solicit artwork from people you know. They are not giving you the work; they simply allow you to use it for the evening. Artwork to display could include drawings, paintings, sculpture, pottery, collage, or any type of art you would like to know. When each person gives you a piece of artwork, be sure to label it in some way. Then write – or print if you don't have great handwriting – the person's name and artwork title onto a blank index card.

Ask people to come by telling people you know about the event. Make flyers to give out at places where you know many people and be sure to tell relatives. On the evening of the event, offer light snacks and lemonade or water for your guests to enjoy somewhere near the artwork.

A couple of days before the event, you will need to empty the room you plan to use. Put the artwork on display and put the name and title cards next to each piece. Anywhere people can come in and out of the in-house art gallery, or the house in general, put a donations bin. As people come by, let them enjoy the art and then ask politely if they would like to donate to the cause before they leave.

Plan a clothing exchange.

A clothing exchange can be beneficial to everyone in your school or worship community! For a clothing exchange, people both give and get gently-used clothes. There are a number of ways to set up this type of activity, but here's the most basic concept.

Find a location to host the clothing exchange. Church fellowship halls and school gyms both make excellent choices. A few days to a week before the event, ask people to bring in their items to donate. Once you collect the items, have someone help you to go through them. Toss anything that is torn, stained, or needs major repair (generally more than re-sewing buttons). Place everything else out on table by sizes and then allow visitors to the exchange to come in to take what they would like.

Make summer pencil packs.

One of the ways that schools help children who come from impoverished homes is to use joint school supplies. When you bring in pencils or folders at the beginning of the school year, they aren't just for you to use. Instead your teacher puts them all together and then everyone gets to use them. While that helps students who cannot afford supplies during the school year, those children have a problem during the summer. They don't have supplies at home!

One way to alleviate this problem is to gather the items to make "summer pencil packs." Research about education shows that students need to work on reading, writing, and math during the summer months to keep from forgetting information. That means that a good pencil pack that has some pencils, erasers, a small notebook, and maybe some math flashcards can go a long way toward helping those students avoid "summer brain drain."

Speak to your school counselor to find out how many children are likely to need a summer pencil pack. Then go to the teachers in your school to tell them about your plan. Ask if they have any pencils, erasers, or leftover notebooks to donate. You may find that you can get many gently used supplies in this way. Once you have what you need, you can solicit donations of small pouches or bags as well as enough supplies to fill the packs. Try asking service groups at churches or local community groups, such as the Kiwanis Club. Even if the group decides not to sponsor your project, individuals in the group may help out.

Once you have the supplies, you will need to package them up. Put a nice note in them to explain their purpose and then ask your school's counselor to give them out to the appropriate students.

Plan a hot chocolate fundraiser.

During the winter months, a hot chocolate fundraiser can help to raise cash quickly! As you head into winter, make sure that you have your supplies ready to go. You will need to have a large thermos or easily portable coffee pot; Styrofoam or other durable cups; cocoa powder and sugar or hot chocolate mix; napkins; and marshmallows.

Determine how much each cup of hot chocolate will cost you. To do that, add up the cost of each item. For example, if you purchase 100 cups for $3, perform this math problem: $3.00/100. Each cup (just the cup – not the hot chocolate) will cost you 3 cents. Once you know the cost of each cup of hot chocolate, you can decide how much you will need to charge per cup to make money. To make it easier, charge something "round" like $1 or $1.50. That means less change you need!

Make dog toys for donations.

The people who work and volunteer at animal shelters often are asking for donations for the animals that are there. Most of those donations are needed items, such as dog bedding, crates, and food. Many dogs really benefit from having toys, too, but it's often something that animal shelter staff members do not have time to solicit. Even if you don't have much money to put into a volunteer project, there are some inexpensive ways to make your own dog toys! Dogs like any type of ball that you can come up with, and ropes with a knot tied at one end usually are great toys. Donating these toys to your local animal shelter can give the dogs there a way to have fun while they wait for a forever home!

Host a tabletop night.

A tabletop night is an inexpensive and easy way to plan something for a community group, church group, or even school. Tabletop games can be board games or card games. Find a place to host the event. It just needs to be a room with a large open space. You will need to put up tables and scatter chairs around the room. Then ask people to show up at the appointed time and bring their own games to play. People can gather around the tables and play the games that look interesting to them. There is no pressure on anyone to stay for any length of time or to "play to win." It's just about playing some games and having an enjoyable evening out with friends.

If you want to make this event a fundraiser, an easy way to do that is to sell drinks and pre-packaged snacks, such as chips and individual snack cakes. Make sure that you are allowed to sell snacks and make signs to let people know how much everything costs. Another idea if the tabletop event is successful is to host the event quarterly so that people can develop relationships with others who enjoy playing games.

Build a game library at children's hospital.

Many children who are at children's hospitals end up there for lengthy stays. Even on the shorter end, being stuck in the hospital for a week can be a frustrating experience, and for kids with long-term diseases like cancer, being in the hospital can be a months-long experience. While many children's hospitals have entertainment areas with gaming consoles, such as the Wii U and xBox One, those hospital wings often don't include a budget to keep the stock updated.

That's where you come in! You can help out by collecting games to help build up the choices available. All large hospitals, and most small ones, have a Volunteer Services department. The people in this department help to coordinate volunteers throughout the hospital. Your first stop will be to contact this person or to have an adult make the initial contact for you. Explain that you would like to build a game library and give this person an idea of your goals, such as how many games and bookshelves you hope to get.

You can raise money through any of the ideas in this book – or come up with your own! – in order to purchase games and bookshelves. Another option is to ask people to donate games they no longer use. Check every game to ensure that it works before putting it in the library. Try to provide manuals if you can, even if that means going online to print the few very important pages letting people know how to play.

Create a labeling system for the games and then put them on the

Learn More: Arbor Day

Arbor Day is one of the only holidays that is celebrated around the globe. The holiday started in Spain in 1805 in a tiny town named Villanueva de la Sierra. It took more than 70 years for the holiday to travel to the United States, where newspaperman J. Sterling Morton hosted the first Arbor Day celebration in Nebraska in 1872.

By 1920, every state in the United States had a certain day designated, or marked, to serve as that state's Arbor Day. Most places around the world celebrate during the planting season, which in North America is during the spring months.

The United States government also set up a national Arbor Day, which is the last Friday of April. The Arbor Day Foundation (http://www.arborday.org) is a nationwide organization that tries to encourage people to plant trees and to raise money for trees and education projects.

bookshelf. The games should be marked to let parents know if they are for younger or older children, or even teenagers. Put together binders of the manuals and ensure that everything has a place on the shelf. Congratulations! Your game library is now complete!

Host an ice cream social at center for people with disabilities.

Many areas of the country still have centers that are for adults who have various physical and mental disabilities. These centers tend not to get as many volunteers heading over as nursing homes and hospitals, but there definitely is a need there as well.

An easy way to get involved at one of these centers for people with disabilities is to host an ice cream social. Doing so is not a difficult task, and the planning should take only a few hours. Contact the center to see if the residents or clients would enjoy such an event and then work out a good time with them. Find out how many people will participate and then plan how much you need in supplies.

Look on the side of a carton of ice cream for the servings per container. It's best to plan to have two servings per person who will be there; you may want to throw in a few extras for staff members who stop by. Then you will need disposable bowls, spoons, and napkins. Stick to simple toppings, such as bottles of caramel and chocolate syrup, whipped cream, and sprinkles. Don't go overboard; limiting the choices will make the process easier for you.

For the day of the event, see if you are able to get one or two friends to accompany with you. Assign each person a part on the ice cream social "assembly line" so that one person is dipping ice cream; one person is doing syrup; and one person is doing other toppings. Be sure to clean up after the social and thank the center for allowing you to come in to be part of their activities schedule.

Provide water for people who are homeless.

Think for a moment about how you feel when you are outside on a hot day and cannot wait to get a cool drink of water. People who are homeless often can find somewhere to go for meals or even to sleep at night but may not be able to get cool water during the day. A simple way for you to help with this process is to get a couple of coolers. Put ice in the coolers and get bottled water in them as well. Head to areas where you know that there is a dense homeless population and just begin to hand out the water.

There is little that you will need to do to spread the word as people generally will come over when they realize that there is someone handing out bottled water. If you enjoy this project, put it on your schedule to do on a regular basis. Perhaps you could go every other Saturday or on Wednesdays. Let friends know and see if you can get others to join you for this simple but wonderful project.

Plan a party fundraiser.

Who doesn't love a party? What if, in addition to having a party, you were able to raise money, too?

Party fundraisers take tons of work, but the payoff usually is pretty good for them. The first task will be to find a place to host a party. If you are thinking small, which is suggested for your first party fundraiser, you could host it at your home. You will need to have an idea of how many people can fit comfortably in the space that you have.

Once you have a space, figure out a budget. The idea with a party fundraiser is that you will have some food and fun activities for the guests, who will pay a fee to come to the party. Light snacks for your friends who come can be done for about $5 per person if you are careful with your shopping. Then you will need to plan for the cost of the entertainment. Playing music could be free, or activities could cost for materials.

Add on to the "entry fee" for each person based on how much you want to raise. Let's look at an example. Pretend you can fit 30 people in your home for a party. Your budget is $8 per person for food and entertainment, and you want to raise $90. Divide the $90 by the 30 guests to learn that you need to bring in $3 per guest. Add that to the $8 budget, and your tickets need to cost $11 in order for you to make your goal.

Make a "Welcome to Our School" day.

It can be tough to come to a new school, but one way that this fear can be alleviated is through having the opportunity to meet other students in a casual setting. In some cases, parents may be part of planning a "welcome" event for new students and parents, but even if they already do something, you can help!

Welcome events are important for elementary, middle, and high school students. For elementary students, the "new kids" are the kindergarten students. Many of them have never been to a formal place like school before, and they may not know what to expect. All you need to do is find out if you can use the school's playground for a Saturday morning a couple of weeks before school begins. Spread the word however you can, such as through a flyer, mailing, or social media. Have parents bring their kindergarten students just to play with others.

Middle and high school "welcome" events may be a bit more structured, but they also should be casual. Again find a time and place to have the event. You can ask people to bring a couple of dollars for pizzas that you order, or you can provide drinks. Then have some students who already go to the school there to talk

about the activities they are in and what they enjoy. Also make sure that
the older students are able to kindly answer any questions that the students new to the school may have for experienced students.

Organize Teacher Appreciation Week.

Teacher Appreciation Week actually is something celebrated the first week of May throughout the United States. There are some inexpensive ways to honor your teachers during this week. Make up a flyer to go out at least two weeks before the event. Each day should have a suggestion for a certain way to celebrate. Some ideas include "bring a piece of fruit," "bring a sweet treat," "give your teacher a card," or "do something nice for a teacher" day. Encourage your fellow students to participate each of the days listed to help honor the teachers at your school.

For a more ambitious project, ask the school's PTA to help honor teachers as well. One way they can do that is to give teachers a gift basket of items that they often need, such as pencils, paper, erasers, markers, and tissues. Offer to help find a few students to coordinate putting together the supply baskets and deliver them to teachers. Be sure to have fellow students write nice notes to the teachers and attach them to the baskets!

Plan a school Beyblade fundraiser.

Although this example is for Beyblades, this type of fundraiser can apply to a whole host of toys or hobbies. This type of fundraiser requires many Beyblade stadia or platforms. Borrow these items from others but be sure to label them so that they can be returned.

The simplest way to plan this fundraiser is a single elimination tournament, but a point-based elimination allows everyone to play multiple times. Depending on the number of people who enter, having each person play three or four initial rounds should work well. People can enter the tournament for a small fee, usually $3-5. Set up a schedule for people who enter to compete against two opponents. Then, make a poster with each competitor's name.

Find volunteers to serve as judges at each competition arena. Record a 1 for a win or a 0 for a loss. Put the scores on the poster and add them up. Allow the top half of competitors to advance. For the championship rounds, pit competitors against each other in no more than four competition arenas at one time to allow others to watch.

Use a single-elimination model for this portion. A competitor advances (wins) or goes home (loses). With any fundraisers of this type you will need to have prizes. Once you know how many competitors you have, budget in some money to purchase small prizes. Alternately you can approach local retailers for gift cards or other small prizes, explaining to them where the money raised from the tournament fundraiser will go.

Plan a rummage sale.

Hosting a rummage sale is a long-standing way to raise cash without spending much (or any) money on the preparations. Find a location to host the fundraiser. You will need to explain where you want the money to go; using the money for a specific project is the best way to convince adults to allow you to use their space. A large open area works best for a rummage sale fundraiser.

When you have a space located, advertise for people to come in to donate their items to the sale. If you are focusing your sale on other children or teens, hit up your friends and expand the circle outward from there. Let's say you are trying to raise money to allow your school's literary team to attend a competition and need $500. Tell your friends. Of course recruit the other students on the literary team. Ask around for items that others will give up for the cause.

The night before the rummage sale, expect to spend many hours sorting and pricing the items. You will need to come armed with plenty of fine-point markers, index cards, and sticker labels. Use them to mark items. When you put the items out on the table, try to sort them by price. Then you can make posters with the prices and put on the tables. People will be able to shop based on their budget.

On the day of the rummage sale, be sure that you have enough volunteers to help you out. There should be people going around to keep everything tidy and put out new items as needed. You also will need people who can carry heavy items out to people's cars. Another donation need is for plastic grocery bags that you can use to help people pack their items in if they purchase several. Be sure to have plenty of change on hand to start the day and have two people staffing the check-out area at all times.

Plan a large upcycling project.

Recycling items that are no longer needed probably is something that you grew up hearing is important. And it is! Sometimes, though, you can make use of recyclable materials, or even trash, in other ways. This process is called "upcycling," and making sculptures is a great way of upcycling while allowing others to enjoy the fruits of your creativity.

Spend some time planning your art project. Use a search engine, such as Google or Bing, to see what others have created. Some people design robots from scrap metal. Others do cool mosaics from bottle caps. There are all kinds of amazing options for recycled or trash art.

Once you know what you plan to do, gather your materials in one spot and get to work! Take your time on the piece of artwork to make sure that you are doing your best work. Also, remember to keep your work area tidy and pick up your materials after each work session.

Take photos of your finished work and print them out. Show them to people who are in charge of the places where you would like to show your work. Ask if you can display the work for a pre-determined amount of time. Promise – and mean it! – that you will pick up the display and restore the area to its former state when the time for the display is over.

Host a food drive.

For your first foray into planning a large-scale project, a food drive is a great place to start. The key to a positive experience planning a food drive is to decide on your audience. A worship group, neighborhood association, or school community is a good place to plan a food drive. Talk to someone at a local food bank first to get a list of the items that they need most desperately and focus your drive on letting people know about those items.

Create a flyer that you will hand out. Ask the person in charge of the host organization to help you plan a way to get the word out in person. Perhaps you could visit Sunday School classes at your church to promote the event. Maybe your neighborhood association secretary would allow you to write an article and put it in the group's newsletter. The school's principal may be willing to put the information in the morning announcements. Get the word out! A food drive is successful only if people know about it!

Set up collection bins and decorate them. The easiest way to get bins is to go to local appliance stores and ask for any large cardboard boxes they have. Use decorative paper to make them look nice and put a clear sign on the box stating that it is for the food drive and the dates of the drive. At the end of the event, have some volunteers help you to bag up the items you collected and deliver them to the food bank.

Make bedtime snack sacks.

There are children who live at homeless shelters, as upsetting as that fact may be. Those children do get an evening meal, but many of them, just like you, would like a snack before bed. That just is not something that most shelters are equipped to handle, however, but you can help with this process by putting together some bedtime snack sacks.

Contact the volunteer coordinator at a local shelter and ask this person how many children typically are staying at the shelter. Once you have that number, you can decide how much you want to commit to this project. Some small shelters may have only three or four children at once while large shelters may have a dozen or more. For our example, let's assume our shelter has five children who live there on average.

Your goal may be to provide bedtime snack sacks for the shelter for one month. (Remember that you can work to keep the project going long-term if you would like.) Five children times 30 days means that you will need 150 snacks, 150 drinks, and 150 bags. (Paper lunch bags are inexpensive and will work.) Use one of the methods already discussed for hosting a drive to get the snacks or ask groups to prepare a certain number of snack sacks. A Girl Scout troop, for example, may be willing to sponsor the bedtime snack sacks for one week of the month. They would provide you with 35 snacks and drinks (5 children x 7 days). Other groups may donate for a week or a couple of days as well. Then you will package up the bedtime snack sacks and take them to the shelter in a large basket. The workers and volunteers there can hand the sacks out each night to the resident children.

Host a coat drive.

A coat drive is best held in the late fall. People will be going through their items to see what no longer fits and will be getting ready to toss out their old items for new ones. That's when you have to pounce! Let people know that you want to collect coats to help people who cannot afford them. Don't focus only on children's coats. Women's and especially men's coats are needed as well. If someone says that he or she does not have an old coat to donate, which often is the case with adults who do not get a new coat each year, ask for a monetary donation.

Take the monetary donations to a local consignment shop to fill in the gaps based on what you have. Get as many coats as you can for the money that you have. The key consideration should be warmth and not whether the coats are trendy because the people who will be wearing them often will be outside for much of the winter. You can find a place to take the coats by calling local shelters or churches with "clothes closets" that they use to give out items to people who need them.

Host a table at a children's festival.

Most mid-sized cities have numerous festivals throughout the year. A growing number of these festivals have children's areas. The idea behind these areas is to give children somewhere to play while adults visit the festival area. You can help out the organizers of a festival you like by offering to host one of these tables. Small festival planners in particular probably are struggling to find enough volunteers to put together and staff these tables, and your offer will be appreciated!

For this project, you will need to put together a small game. Don't worry about prizes. Just put together something simple and fun. It could be offering chalk for sidewalk art or having jump ropes available for a play area. Anything that will give kids a few minutes of entertainment is your only goal in coming up with something to do.

Next, find some volunteers! Ask your friends and family to come help you with staffing your table at the festival. For most activities, you will need at least two people at all times. Don't forget to create a schedule for everyone and to give yourself a chance to eat lunch and have a small break at some point during the day. Be sure to check in with your volunteers a couple of days before the event to make sure that they still plan to attend.

Organize a babysitting brigade.

Offering to help a family that needs a babysitter in a crisis situation, such as a when a parent has surgery, is a great way to help out. If you know of a family that may have longer-term needs, though, organizing a babysitting brigade takes this idea a step further. When a family has a long-term need, talk to an adult about whether they could use babysitting help. Get a basic schedule down. Perhaps a family that loses a member could benefit from someone watching the younger kids once a week for a respite, or a family with a parent who gets cancer may need help on days that parent has chemotherapy. Sit down and work out this calendar.

Use the calendar to begin to find people you know who babysit who can fill in. There are a number of wonderful websites, such as

CaringBridge.com, that make it simple to create a calendar and give others the information to sign in. Ask only people you know who will be respectful and responsible, and you will be doing a wonderful service for a family in need!

Other Resources

For easier access to these links, visit BrandiBrownOnline.com and look for the "Volunteer Links" tab.

Zoom into Action: Family Guide to Volunteering
This PDF guide is a 16-page booklet that will help you to decide the best volunteer projects for you.

http://www-tc.pbskids.org/zoom/grownups/action/pdfs/volunteer_guide.pdf

ASPCA: Get Involved

The American Society for the Prevention of Cruelty of Animals has plenty of ideas to help get started helping animals.

https://www.aspca.org/get-involved

FoodPantries.org

Use this interactive map to find food pantries in your area.

http://www.foodpantries.org/

FeedingAmerica.org

This website contains scores of links for ways to help advocate for better options for low-income families and to begin to help people who need food.

http://www.feedingamerica.org/take-action/

65 Ways Students Can Change Schools

This article has plenty of food for thought on ways that students can help to make their schools better places. Get plenty of ideas to get started here!

http://www.soundout.org/article.115.html

Creative Ways to Help Our Schools

This article really is geared toward adults who are interested in large time commitments in their schools, but it may spark some ideas for ways you can help, too.

http://www.youthworkers.net/index.cfm/fuseaction/blog.view/BlogID/98

Volunteer as a Family

Learn why you should volunteer as a child and what you can get out of the experience.

http://www.unitedway.org/take-action/volunteer-as-a-family

Tips for Volunteering with Kids

Have an adult read through this article before you volunteer together! It includes tips for adults who are going to go to volunteer opportunities with children helping out.

http://www.pbs.org/parents/special/article-tips-for-volunteering-with-kids.html

Fundraising Ideas for Kids

Here are a few ideas for fundraisers that children are able to do.

http://www.better-fundraising-ideas.com/fundraising-ideas-for-kids.html

50 Fundraising Ideas

Get started with these ideas. Let them spark your imagination for the fundraising idea that will work best for your school or community.

http://www.signupgenius.com/nonprofit/50-creative-and-easy-fundraising-ideas.cfm

Family Homelessness Facts

Read through this article and the facts it includes to help you understand the struggles that await homeless families in the United States.

http://www.greendoors.org/facts/family-homelessness.php

11 Facts about Homeless Teens

About one-third of people who are homeless are less than 24 years old. Find out more about them!

https://www.dosomething.org/facts/11-facts-about-homeless-teens

16 Ways Kids Can Help with Thanksgiving Dinner

These ideas are ways that children can help their own families and communities out in preparing for Thanksgiving dinner. Just because the help may go to family doesn't mean that it doesn't count! Try offering to do one of these jobs for your family to help take the pressure off the Thanksgiving Day hosts.

https://www.care.com/a/16-ways-kids-can-help-with-thanksgiving-dinner-1309050937

Top 10 Reasons to Volunteer

Learn some of the ways that volunteer helps not just the person benefiting from the work but also volunteers and the community at large.

https://students.ucsd.edu/student-life/involvement/community/reasons.html

Benefits of Volunteering

In addition to the joy of helping out, you can boost your chances for getting into honor societies, landing cool summer jobs, and securing spots in colleges with your volunteer record.

http://www.worldvolunteerweb.org/resources/how-to-guides/volunteer/doc/benefits-of-volunteering.html

About the Author

Brandi Brown started her life as a volunteer when she was just a child, helping her mother plan her school's Halloween carnival. In high school, she started two student organizations, served on the Student Council, and volunteered through her church's youth group. As an adult, volunteering has been a huge part of Brandi's life, and she now enjoys taking her children along with her.

Brandi lives in Raleigh, North Carolina with her husband and 2 children. She enjoys reading, going to festivals, and trying out new hobbies with her family.

You can follow Brandi on Twitter @SpeaksBrandi, on Facebook at https://www.facebook.com/BrandiLeighBrown. Check out her website at www.brandibrownonline.com.